I0014484

Affiliate Marketing and Success Systems

Tips and secrets to maximize your success

IQ PRESS, INC.

<u>Disclaimer</u>

CONTENTS

ACKNOWLEDGMENTS

IQ Press, Inc. is a small publishing company dedicated to providing access to educational materials primarily in small business start-up and development. Their mission is to bring the reader useful information that can be implemented with a small capital outlay and generate income streams for the reader to implement.

We hope you enjoy these reports and that they will help improve your life.

www.IQPress.org

CHAPTER 1 - EARNING MONEY WITH NICHE AFFILIATE MARKETING

Affiliate marketers with experience know that affiliate money is made by finding a niche market that's profitable. Then you take advantage of it. If you aren't able to find a niche market, your income as an affiliate marketer is going to suffer significantly. Since your business needs income to survive, this is a critical component for anyone that plans to earn money as an affiliate marketer.

You can find the right market just by taking the time to do some research. There are plenty of niche markets. You just have to match the right niche market for you. Once you do this you'll be able to generate an income stream that will pleasantly surprise you. Now that you know how important it is to find that niche market, let's look at the steps that will help you identify the right niche for your business.

1. You need to identify an affiliate market that you are interested in and it's always best if you have knowledge in the niche. Initially look for a broad category such as health

and fitness. Once you have the main category, you will drill down until you find that niche that's just right for you.

Investigate these small components available within the market. For example, let's say the main category is golf. You might identify the niche within the golf market as golf tees or golf shirts. You can break it down even further into different types of shirts.

Once you are able to recognize your niche you need to find an affiliate product that fits within that niche. There are a number of marketplace sites that have many affiliates on them. Clickbank is one of those sites. With your niche in hand, you can search for matching products on these sites and then apply to be an affiliate. Once accepted it's time to get busy marketing.

One word of advice: When you begin to search for your niche keep in mind that different products will pay different commissions so don't grab the first niche match you find. Instead spend some time going through the products you are looking for to find the highest paying ones.

Earning money with niche affiliate marketing is the fastest way to become involved with internet marketing. It makes it easy to promote the product(s) you have for sale, it makes it easier to choose keywords, and it makes it easier to target traffic when you are focused. Why wait any longer? Why not enjoy what so many others are already enjoying? Earn income now.

Revenue Generation With Affiliate Programs

There are few projects no matter what size they are, that don't require a number of steps to reach completion and more importantly success. This is also true when you want to enjoy revenue generation through affiliate programs. The process of making yourself stand out from others marketing the same products as yourself is one of those cases where you will need to implement a number of steps. In fact, here are a few steps that will help you reach the success you desire.

You Need Your Own Site

There's no point in even looking at affiliate marketing until you have your website up and running. This is critical since traffic that reaches your site are potential customers, and your goal is marketing your products and convert that traffic into sales.

The products you offer may be just those of an affiliate (or you may be combining your own product lines with an affiliate), but you will be providing direct links to the affiliates. When those links are clicked and a purchase is completed the affiliate records that sale and you have earned a commission.

Once your site is up and running, you need to create your ads. This is a key component that you will need to focus your attention on. Most affiliates provide you with a full set of ads that you can use, both banner or rectangle style and word text ads. However, designing your own ads will have far more impact when done correctly. That's because people become immune to ads, especially ones they repeatedly see, which commonly occurs with the larger affiliates.

The better solution is to contact the affiliate asking if it's okay to create your own ads. Once you have received the okay you can begin work to create ads that will encourage visitors to click and see what the ad has to offer.

It's always better if you also have at least a few products of your own available to mix with the affiliates products. It's always wise to have at least a handful of products that aren't easily found on other affiliate sites. The reason for this is so that the traffic that comes to your site arrives there because you have something they can't find on another site. It also helps you to build a solid market segment.

You need to build a solid relationship with those people who become customers and who are already customers. Finally, don't try to market all the products at once. With many of the affiliate services, you could find yourself overwhelmed, and trying to market too many products. Find your niche and stick to it.

Chapter 2 - How to Create a Product and Make Your Own Automated Income Website

If you want an automated income system you can start searching online and find one that you think will do well based on your research, become an affiliate, and start marketing that product focusing on creating an automated income system. However, there's another way to create an automated income and that's to create your own product.

Create a Hot Topic

If you create a marketable product, such as a "how to make money," book all the profits will go to your pocket, rather than getting a percentage from someone else's marketable product. And here is the real kicker – now you can be the vendor offering an affiliate program, and you can make money from others who are selling your product(s).

So take some time and do your homework to learn what it is internet users are looking for. Then build your product around that. If you want to create a book, but you are not a writer there are many services online where you can hire a writer to put together your book.

Generate Traffic

Once you've created your product you'll need to generate traffic. Pick one method of generating traffic and focus on it. You can expand later but otherwise your time will be too spread out, and none of the traffic generation sources are getting your full attention.

Giving something away is a good way to bring people to your site. For example, a free report or a video that provides the viewer with ideas and ways to start their own automated income website. A monthly newsletter is another great giveaway. That's just a couple of ideas. Next you'll need to convert your visitors.

Building the Conversion System

The first thing you need to factor into your plan is how you are going to generate leads. With a low cost report the use of a squeeze page might not make sense. Even when you are paying your affiliate 100% they still may not be happy with a squeeze page. Instead you can use an exit popup to operate the free report. A squeeze page that looks like a membership signup page always works well.

Once you have a list of those people who have signed up you can easily follow up offering them great content, while you build a relationship with them and therefore increase your conversion rate.

Once you know how you are going to capture leads, it's time to start working on your sales page. If you have a really HOT topic it won't take much to convince visitors to your page to make the purchase.

There are three things every sales page must include, which is what you are offering, what they will get, and how they are able to get it. Remember, keep it simple and to the point. That's it in a nutshell. Of course, one short article can't give you all the detail but you are certainly ready to get started and there's plenty of excellent information online.

Successfully Automate Your Income Online

Are you looking for an opportunity to make money without having to work full time? You'll be glad to know there are a number of excellent opportunities. Just make sure you avoid those "get rich quick schemes" that are floating around. There are several excellent ways to break away from the day-to-day grind and begin to earn a comfortable living working online only a few hours a week once your business is established.

So here's a question for you. If you were naturally wealthy what would you do with your time? I bet the list is long. Whether you travel, spend more time with your children, or enjoy your hobby, once you have your automated income business up and running, you'll be able to do the things you wish you had time for now.

When you are looking for an automated income opportunity there are a few things you should consider:

* Look for affiliate products that are in demand currently
* Once you have a short list, look for those that offer the best pay
* Finally, choose something that interests you, that you believe in – it will make marketing that much easier. This can sometimes take a while – take your time – embrace your choices to create a site of value and therefore generate automated income

Once you've identified your calling and found the right affiliate for yourself it's time to move to the next step in successfully automating your income.

Learn to Generate Value

Once you generate traffic and they arrive at your blog or site, they will only stay or return if you have something of value that you can offer them. This means that you need to incorporate your conversion into your automated income online affiliate program. You can do this by giving away something.

Visitors like free things. Give them a report, a video, a newsletter, etc. There are all kinds of things you can do to make your site valuable. The goal here is to create a list of potential customers by having the visitor sign up to receive the free item, which gives you access to their email address.

Automated Income Stream

Early on you are going to be putting in a lot of time to get your business off the ground. Anyone who tells you that you'll be wealthy overnight isn't being honest. But here's the deal – once you have put the time in, you've generated traffic to your site, created your sales page, and are converting your traffic to sales, you can sit back and relax while you watch the money pour in. The only question left is what are you waiting for?

The Three Most Important Affiliate Marketing Tips That Affiliate Marketers Should Know About

Being an affiliate marketer gives you a license to make money. Once you understand how it all works and you know what you need to do you'll be enjoying significant earnings. Here are three of the most important affiliate marketing tips that you need to know. They'll help you make money online, and ensure you can carry that revenue through into the future.

Learn Technical Basics

Without a technical background you are at a disadvantage over those with a technical background, but don't let that stop you. You don't have to be a top-notch programmer, but you do need to learn a little of the basics when it comes to html, and basic php scripts. The biggest area of trouble is when something goes awry and you don't have the basics to even figure out what has gone wrong. It won't take you long to learn the basics if you just set your mind to it. Do a quick

Google search and you'll find all kinds of tutorials that can help you.

Hone Your Writing Skills

You need to know how to write. If you think that you already know how to write, you probably do. But the question is do you know how to write content for a website? Great writing skills will get your blog better reviews. Good writing will get your site ranked better and it will bring relevant traffic to your site. Strong writing will be your best friend – it will help to generate sales. When your site or blog begins to generate traffic you will earn revenue as an affiliate marketer.

Test, Test and Test

Next you need to test then you need to test some more. You need to run many different variations and test each one of them. If you don't do this you will have no idea what is actually producing for you. This includes the testing of landing pages, headlines, keywords, ad copy, and the list goes on.

An affiliate marketer who is failing simply means they didn't do the testing they needed to do. Yes you might have to spend a little money and you'll have to invest time, but in the end it will enable you to make a lot of money.

Becoming an affiliate marketer that is generating significant revenue is not as difficult as you might think. Incorporating these three tips into your overall strategy will bring you that much closer to reaching your goal of financial wealth.

Making Easy Money Using Affiliate Marketing

Affiliate marketing is simply a way to generate income online. You as a publisher for a company's products pay for marketing the products or services they offer. There are all kinds of ways that products, services, or websites can be promoted. In affiliate marketing you as the publisher are paid a commission when a visitor clicks through a link on your website or blog that takes that visitor to another site where they buy products or services.

Commissions are usually calculated as a percentage, however, occasionally they are a fixed rate per conversion. Conversions are tracked a few ways. The most common is that you receive your own code that identifies you. When you place the links on your site this code is embedded in those links, which allows the advertiser to monitor the conversions and pay the appropriate publishers the appropriate amount of money.

Another option is the publisher pays a commission when you refer a visitor and that visitor acts in some manner. For example, he/she signs up for a newsletter and gives their email address, or completes an online survey and gives his/her name and address.

Sometimes the advertiser provides you the publisher a coupon code that you will provide to your visitors and the advertiser will track payments appropriately. Of course, that's the short of it all. It's a little more in-depth than this, but that gives you an understanding of how it all comes together.

Amazon was one of the first to implement an affiliate marketing program. There were others back then but none were anywhere near the size of Amazon. They began their affiliate program in 1996 and today they generate billions of dollars in sales through their affiliate program.

Today, e-commerce is huge online, and affiliate marketing is just as large. In 2006 affiliate marketers generated an estimated 7 billion dollars in sales and it's estimated that number has now doubled. There is tons of easy money to be made online through affiliate marketing. The only question is will you recognize the potential here and enjoy the revenue, or will you miss out on an excellent opportunity.

Chapter 3 - Affiliate Marketing 101 - Earn Real Income

If you are new to affiliate marketing you may feel overwhelmed when you first look at affiliate marketing. However, it's not nearly as difficult as you might think. To start your affiliate marketing business, you don't need to understand all the techniques right away.

You will become proficient at the various methods over time. Affiliate marketing can offer you a real income, and once your business is established you'll have to put in very little time to maintain your income. There is no limit on how much money your business can make as an affiliate.

What's really nice about affiliate marketing is that you can scale it to whatever size you want. There are only two requirements for your affiliate marketing site to succeed. They are traffic and pre-selling copywriting.

Once you get targeted traffic to your site, making the sale becomes much easier. Don't complicate the process. It doesn't require all kinds of fancy strategies or huge budgets. There are three strong methods to use to build your affiliate marketing business.

1. List Building

You may have already heard of list building. This is a technique that has resulted in millions of dollars in profits being generated. For link building to be successful you need to bring traffic to your page. You then convert those visitors to subscribers. You attract new subscribers by offering something of value to your targeted visitors. You can offer to give away free things like videos or reports.

2. Build a Loyal Following and Recommend Specific Products

You can build a loyal following with a blog or with your newsletter. You can review products and then recommend them to your following either in your newsletter or through your blog.

3. Create a Website That's About Reviews

This is considered the fastest way to use affiliate marketing to earn money. It's quite a simple concept. A review site is an excellent way to promote the affiliate products. You don't have to offer just one product on your website. You can offer as many products as you like. Your reviews should include what you like, what you dislike, and how it has been a benefit to you. Then you just place your affiliate link and begin to enjoy the revenue it generates.

Can a Beginner Make Real Money as an Affiliate?

Yes beginners can make money with affiliate marketing. You can work your way up to a full time income in no time at all. You can enjoy a reasonable salary, become more experienced, and grow your income. There's the potential to enjoy full time income through affiliates. Take advantage of this terrific earning opportunity.

Six Tips to Choose the Right Affiliate Program

There are thousands upon thousands of affiliate programs to choose from, so how do you know which is the right choice if you want to make money. Follow these tips to help you choose the right money making affiliate program.

Affiliates are an excellent way to make money online. In fact, when done right you can enjoy a full time income, even growing wealth. There's no need to have to come up with your own product, your own ads, or anything else. The affiliate will provide you with all of this. If your site already has high traffic then you are sitting in a nice position to generate a steady flow of income. If not, you will need to work on this part of your money-making strategy.

1. Match Content to Your Site

To enjoy the highest revenue choose an affiliate that matches the products you sell on your site. At the very least try to add a product that compliments your niche.

2. Highest Commission

Choose an affiliate program that pays a good commission. For example, choose an affiliate that pays 30% to 50% over an affiliate that pays 10%.

3. Trust

You want to be associated with an affiliate program where you can trust the vendor and you can trust the product(s) you are going to be marketing. It's much easier to write sales copy if you know you are promoting great products.

4. Pay Schedules

Before you join any affiliate program, you should examine the pay schedule and ensure you will be paid at least monthly. You should also check what the minimum payment is. For example, some will have a $25 minimum payment while others may have a $100 minimum. Make sure you are okay with whatever that threshold is.

5. Tracking

The affiliate program you choose should include proper tracking tools so you can track your earning to learn where you are strong, where you are weak, and what you need to tweak.

6. Customer Support

You want to know that if you have affiliate troubles you can reach someone for assistance. You might be surprised to learn just what a rarity this is these days. Nothing's more frustrating than not being able to get answers.

Affiliate programs have the opportunity to make money. Done right you can make tons of money, and enjoying the wealth you've dreamed of.

A Proven Strategy for Quick Earnings With Affiliate Marketing

For those of you not familiar with affiliate marketing, it's definitely one of the best ways to enjoy significant earnings online. If you are new to earning online you'll want to consider affiliate marketing. Let's look at some of the benefits of affiliate marketing.

1. You don't have to tie money up in inventory, creating and designing product packaging, or any of the other costs associated with bringing a product to market. The vendor is responsible for all of this including stocking the products so you have no large cash outlay.

2. By promoting the vendor's products you save all kinds of money. Your overhead costs are minimal, your profits high, and you can enjoy quick earnings.

3. You are not responsible for warranties, returns, customer service, etc. That's all the responsibility of the vendor.

Choosing the Product Will Sell

1. While it's always important to look for a niche that interests you, there are three products that consistently do well. These are dating products, weight loss products, and money making products.

2. Once you have determined what your niche will be, use Google, and search for products. Use the keywords you would have used if you were shopping for that product.

3. Go through your search results searching the websites for valuable content. Read the product reviews and if there are any YouTube videos be sure to watch them.

4. Once you have narrowed down your list, sign up for free things, newsletters, emails, etc. Then decide if this is the right affiliate for you.

Build Your Site

Once you have chosen your affiliate you will:

1. Build your site

2. Begin to add content in the form of blog posts. Do your research. You want to sound knowledgeable about the products you are promoting.

3. Create an autoresponder series of newsletters, emails, sales, etc. Make sure they are spaced out well. You don't want to overwhelm your potential customers.

4. Now you need to drive traffic to your site. There are many techniques you can use to accomplish this. Keywords, search engine optimization, and PPC are a few ways to bring traffic to your site.

5. Remember to utilize social media, which is an excellent way to attract new followers, and build your name in the industry.

6. Spend about 25% of your time reading and learning about internet marketing, and more importantly affiliate marketing.

Put this proven affiliate strategy into play and you will be enjoying earnings in no time at all

Generate Revenue With Affiliate Marketing Programs

The internet offers all kinds of e-commerce opportunities. If you are starting your own online business the fastest way to enjoy revenue generation is to begin with an affiliate marketing program.

What is Affiliate Marketing?
Affiliate marketing is simply when you promote another company's products or services and for doing that you are paid a commission. Affiliate marketing is highly profitable and you can make significant revenue once you master affiliate marketing techniques.

What is the Process to Start Your Own Affiliate Marketing Business?
It begins with you signing up with an affiliate company online. Starting to generate income is pretty easy and relatively fast. Find an affiliate program that you feel fits your

company then sign up, which is almost always free. There are a number of companies that are sites where you can sign up for many affiliates.

Once you sign up to be an affiliate for the company, you may have to wait for their approval. After you've received the approval you can begin to market their products and/or services. If you are using an affiliate marketing site like Clickbank you can start to look through the categories to find a niche that's right for your company. Finding the right product is really

Once you've found the affiliate with the right match of products or services it's time to get the affiliate link, which is a link that has a special code that's your unique identifier. This is what the company will use to track your commissions. Affiliate links can be text links or they can be banners.

Once you have your affiliate links it is time to begin to promote the products and/or services you have chose. The link you provide will recommend the purchasing of these products or services. You will include the affiliate link in your message to the client, or you will have it on your sales page where it automatically redirects to the affiliates website. If they purchase the products and/or services you earn yourself a nice commission.

Different companies pay different commission rates to their affiliates, so when you are looking to choose the affiliate you want to promote make sure you keep this in mind. It should be part of your decision making process.

That's really all there is to affiliate marketing. It's an easy way to start your own online business and generate revenue from these incomes streams, which will grow exponentially with the right marketing plan. Why wait? Why not see what kind of revenue you can generate with affiliate marketing?

Making an Automated Income Stream Work for You

Automated Income Stream was actually created by Chris Cobb, who has a reputation for successful creations. Cobb launched "Millionaire Mastermind," a solid system for generating leads. This has help tons of people and today there are all kinds of internet marketers in the industry now thanks to Cobb. Today there are a number of automated income stream opportunities.

When you invest in an automated income stream system can provide you with guidance. This is extremely helpful for most of us who simply don't have the necessary experience to undertake such a venture all on our own. Membership programs can be very beneficial because there goal is to train other internet marketers so they can be successful too. Membership can also be beneficial to those already established.

Membership can provide all kinds of communication with others in the same field, but it also offers a great deal more such as manuals and audio training sessions. Cris Cobb's automated income stream offers a program that affiliate marketers should be able to benefit from.

He will teach things such as how you can put together a solid opt-in list, how to move towards success with Google AdWords quicker, and how to generate revenue using several different methods, rather than just focusing on one kind of internet marketing. Cobb's step by step guide covers even the smallest detail, as it walks you through how to create a successful online marketing business. It's not about learning it all overnight. Instead, the learning process is spread over time. If you were hoping to become successful fast, don't underestimate the power of giving your growth the time it needs and your learning curve as well. After all, you want to put the time in during the beginning and then sit back and enjoy the revenue later with only a minimal time investment.

There are a number of excellent methods to create an automated income stream. There are all kinds of opportunities online that are being overlooked by many, who simply find themselves overwhelmed by the complexity of the internet, which by the way isn't nearly as complex as you may think.

Still others find themselves parted from their money by some convincing snake oil salesmen who claims to have the answers to "getting rich overnight," on the internet. If it sounds too good to be true it is. Remember there are many excellent legitimate ways to create an automated income stream that work well so take advantage, and start to change your life for the better.

Chapter 4 - How to Build an Automated Income System

You've probably seen those ads yourself – products that claim to bring thousands of daily visitors to your site and make you millions of dollars. Do you find yourself asking if that were true, why would they be selling it to you? That's a common question and the answer is there's a great deal of money to be made in selling the "how to build an automated income system." In fact, there's more money to be made this way than actually using the plan.

This is just another way to grow wealth online. Selling software and information are the two fastest ways to take your monthly income from zero to thousands in no time at all. Regardless of the product(s) the marketing formula remains the same: Traffic plus conversion equals sales.

There are tons of ways to bring traffic to your site, but there's only one strategy that lets you use all of them at once. Let's first look at conversion rates, which is the percentage of visitors to your page that take action such as making a purchase, joining a mailing list, or signing up for an affiliate product.

Now let's look at traffic to your site. There are hundreds of methods to generate traffic to your site including:

* Banner ads

* Pay-Per-Click ads

* Ezine ads

* Article marketing

* Social marketing

* Video marketing

* Press releases

* Blogging

* Webinars

And that's just a handful of the most common. Look for the methods that will benefit your business the most. It takes a great deal of time to initially learn how to generate traffic and then to make your traffic generation work.

Finally, let's look at how to set up your automated income system.

1. Buy the rights or create an information product on a topic that's currently hot. This can change over time so always be

on the lookout for the most current hot product to ensure your income isn't interrupted.

2. Build your conversion system, which might include a squeeze page, follow-ups, and a sales page.

3. Get others to sell the product and then split the profits with them, or you will sell someone else's product. If you have your own product that you've designed you'll be the vendor looking for affiliates. If you are going to market another vendor's product, which is the quickest and easiest method, then you'll be the affiliate.

You can run your automated income system business from home with only a small amount of intervention from you, so expect to put only a few hours a week into your business once it is up and running.

Chapter 5 - Can You Become Wealthy With Affiliate Marketing?

It is a common mistake to get involved with affiliate marketing with the belief that in no time at all you'll be sitting on a tropical beach drinking margaritas. This illusion is thanks to a lot of overzealous hype, and far too many get rich schemes that are circulating online.

The truth is you can become wealthy with affiliate marketing, but you are not going to do it overnight, and you are going to have to invest some time initially. In other words, like everything in life, if you put the necessary work and effort into it then you will reap the benefits. The money is there just waiting to be made, but it takes time and effort.

Affiliate marketing is a business, and that's how it needs to be treated if you want to enjoy success and wealth. Every day you will need to put time in building your targeted traffic and promoting your product(s).

In the early stages, you can expect your commission checks will be relatively small. As you garner skills selling online and your skills improve on how to gain targeted traffic, close an online sale, and compel visitors to want to buy your product, you will see your revenue grow.

You need to be realistic in the early stages. For example, set a goal of $1200 to $1600 to be earning per month within the first six months. If you put the work into your affiliate marketing, you can easily reach that target much sooner than six months. Continue to set goals and as you meet them increase them. Like any business, your site will grow and your revenues will grow with time. Building a solid platform will allow you to enjoy revenue from the affiliate program for years to come.

When you are building your affiliate marketing business be patient. Feeling frustrated is common, especially in the early stages when you are working so hard and seeing so little in the way of returns. If you are using proven affiliate marketing methods then it will all come together. Soon you will be enjoying the benefits of all your hard work.

Once your affiliate marketing business is established you'll be able to relax putting in far fewer hours. In many cases all that's needed is a couple of hours a week. It is at this stage you will begin to build your wealth and enjoy it.

Can you become wealthy with affiliate marketing? Absolutely! The key is time and patience.

The Truth About Affiliate Marketing Earnings

If you've been searching for opportunities to make money online, you've likely come across affiliate marketing. You may have heard both good and bad when it comes to affiliate marketing. Affiliate marketing is complex yet it runs of the simplest business model. It's time you learned the truth about affiliate marketing and potential earnings.

Affiliate marketing is a bit hard to understand but there is plenty of help available online so don't let the initial overwhelming feelings stop you from progressing with affiliate marketing and enjoying the earnings potential affiliate marketing presents.

It begins with deciding what it is you want to promote and sell as an affiliate. This is the biggest step and it requires a great deal of time and work determining what the best niche market for you to go after. After you've created a short list determine which product is likely to get the most traffic to your site.

The internet is continuously changing so your research will be an ongoing process. There are hundreds of affiliates to choose from and there are also the memberships at sites like Clickbank. It's work – then again if it were a breeze why would anyone show up at their 9 to 5 job when they could just make a million with affiliates.

When you put yourself in the right state of mind, you'll be able to find your niche markets. Put simply a niche market is the determining the market that you'll find lucrative. In other words before you make your final decision about what your niche will be you need to make sure that there are enough potential buyers and that there is not too much competition.

Keyword research will give you the answers you need. Keyword research can be tedious. Google offers a free keyword tool. You want to find the keywords that are searched the most. Then you can finalize your niche market decision.

Don't go spending hundreds of dollars to take an affiliate marketing course. There's a lot of free information available online. Explore what's out there. If you still feel you'd benefit from an affiliate marketing course, then go ahead and invest. Most affiliates are also provided with help and are there to assist you when you need it.

Becoming an affiliate marketer is really exciting and the earning potential is enough to entice you into exploring this income opportunity further. While there are a number of opportunities to make money online, affiliate marketing requires no investment and promises excellent earnings.

Methods to Automate Your Income Stream

There are a number of methods to automate your income stream. We can just touch on your options in this article. There are a number of books on the market that go into great detail.

First, you need to create your business. This isn't as terrifying as some think. You'll need a computer, an internet connect, a printer, and a product to sell. Next set up your website. Operating a website based business is the cheapest business you can ever own, with few hassles. Creating an automated income source initially takes hard work but after its set up the maintenance is minimal. There's no rent to pay, no office furniture to buy, no need for a lot of space.

Buying a domain, getting hosting, hiring a web designer, getting your site optimized for better placement, and purchasing CPC ads should cost you less than $1000, even less if you do your own web design.

There are a number of ways to automate your income. You can turn the service you provide into a product such as an e-book or DVD. Invest your time once and then after that you can automate your income. You can mass-produce this stuff for a very low cost.

Rather than an informational product, you could sell a "product" such as exercise equipment or some new type of gadget. If you are automating your income, you do not want to be the one that is filling and shipping the orders. The way to avoid this is by finding a solid affiliate(s). The affiliate will fill the orders and you will fill your bank account.

When done right you'll invest only a couple of hours a week while the money grows in your bank account. You can quit your job and spend your time sipping margaritas on a tropical beach.

What is an Automated Income Stream and Does it Work?

An automated income stream means the income never stops, all the while you are doing minimal work. Many approach the automated income stream with doubt. So does it really work? Is certainly does, providing you choose your automated income stream wisely.

If you find yourself invited to a get rich overnight offer you can bet it doesn't work. Like with anything in life there is no easy way to make money quickly. But what a legitimate automated income stream does is offer you an ongoing income and the wealth you desire.

You need to find the right affiliate for your website or blog. You also need to choose an affiliate for your automated income stream that's legitimate. Don't get involved with a get rich scheme. Remember, if it sounds too good to be true it will be. Instead, look for a sound affiliate that will offer you an automated income stream for years to come, allowing you to build the wealth you've been looking for.

It starts with you putting in the work, the time, and the effort. Once you've established your income stream you can relax. You'll need to put in a few hours a week to keep things going. If you have not been making money through your online ventures then you are doing something wrong. It's time to make a change and focus your attention on a different passion – an automated income stream.

Sometimes you might feel totally lost or out of sync. Don't' worry, you aren't alone. Don't get too frustrated. There's plenty of help online, and good affiliates have all the help you'll ever need, so don't be afraid to ask. Once you have all the knowledge you need things will go smoothly and you'll enjoy a monthly revenue stream.

Your mind is powerful so put it to work. The opportunities online have barely been touched. So don't be afraid to take the power of the internet to the next level. While the gurus claim to share their secrets don't be surprised to learn that the most important secrets they keep to themselves.

You were smart enough to recognize that there is an opportunity to develop an automated income stream, so you are certainly smart enough to think past the information you are given and create your own wealth once you have the template.

Do your research, choose your affiliate, implement the plan, think outside the box, work hard at first, and relax allot once your automated income stream is established.

Chapter 6 - Using Your Website to Promote Affiliates and Make Money

An affiliate marketer is someone who promotes the product(s) of a vendor who will also have a website where these products are sold. When a visitor from your website clicks the link, arrives on the vendor's website, and completes a purchase, you will be paid a commission. There are a number of business models that are utilized when it comes to generating profits through affiliate marketing. There's certainly no question that this is an opportunity to make money.

How Hard is Setting up an Affiliate Marketer?

If you are new to the online world of e-commerce it may seem a little overwhelming and it may be frustrating at times. However, you can do this. If you run into trouble ask questions. There are many excellent forums out there and some are worth joining. If you aren't sure how to do something then copy someone who is being successful. And most of all don't give up. Just chug along slowly and you'll be surprised to discover just how fast you learn how to operate smoothly.

What Should You Sell?

You will need to decide what product(s) you want to promote. It's always best if you can find a niche market to work in, because there will be more money to make. You can market one or more products and you can market from more than one vendor. There are several marketplaces where you can find all kinds of vendors to choose from. Clickbank is just one example. Most of these sites are fairly easy to navigate around in.

What is the Role of Your Website?

There are different ways you can promote your affiliate products. One of the most popular methods is using email or social media networks like Facebook. You don't need to have your own site, but if you do there's other opportunities available to you and it makes it that much easier to extend your reach that much further.

Earlier it was harder to design and build a website. But now it's not nearly as daunting sincere there are all kinds of software to help you quickly put together a fantastic looking website without having any understanding of HTML. There are all kinds of templates to choose from that are professional eliminating the need to hire a professional to design a professional looking site.

Running an online business is not nearly as difficult as it may seem. Using your website to promote affiliates is an easy way to make money. Over time you can turn affiliate marketing into your full time job.

How to Select the Right Affiliate Program for Success

Even when you select an affiliate program that offers high quality products or services, this is no guarantee that you will be successful. Just ask the thousands who have failed with some of the largest box stores. It's a bit like having the very best plane but without a trained pilot, the plane will go nowhere. You need to have the right training to ensure you choose the right affiliate for you.

You need to take some time to know the business you are considering becoming an affiliate for. You also need to evaluate your own business and yourself. Be honest here, because if you are you will enjoy affiliate success. Just having a desire to make money through an affiliate program is not enough to make it happen.

There's a river of gold flowing through every corner of the internet. However, to access it and enjoy that same income others are enjoying you need to combine you being trained with the best affiliate program. So don't look for the right affiliate program unless you've received the guidance and training you need.

There are plenty of affiliates that seem to share one factor – they are the equivalent of the local hustler. In fact, many people associate affiliates with the hustler. This isn't how the majority of affiliates are. The is a huge number of affiliate marketing programs and endless opportunities so take the time to make a good match and find the right affiliate program for success.

Start by asking yourself what is the best affiliate program for the niche market I'm working in. Start by asking yourself what visitors come to your site to buy. Choose affiliate programs that match the niche market you already have. Make a short list and then you will need to research the affiliates you are considering.

Look at how these affiliate programs are rating, what their conversion rate looks like, how often affiliates get paid, what the success rate is for those affiliates who are promoting the product. There are a number of sites that promote tons of affiliates. It's a great way to be able to choose one or more affiliate programs easily and simplify the payment process.

* Commission Junction
* Google Affiliate Network
* Linkshare
* Clickbank
* Wolfstorm Media

That's a short list of the sites offering affiliates, but it's a great place to start.

How to Automate Your Income Sit Back and Relax

Instead of busting your butt every day to earn money, why not work hard once and build your income stream, then sit back and relax with only minimal work to maintain it. Putting your income on autopilot really does work. Let's look at how to do that.

Simplify
Simplification is king, whether it's your kitchen cupboards or your to-do-list, or anything else in your life the more you eliminate clutter, the simpler your life will become and the less stress you will find yourself dealing with.

Income Concepts

There are several concepts that are relevant to income earning, yet most are seldom thought about. The majority of us work jobs where we put in the hours and then get a check on payday that allows us to live the lifestyle we choose. Some of us have to work two jobs to save money or pay off debt. That's all okay, except if you are tired of having no control over your earning potential then now is a good time for a change. If you put that same energy into your own business, you could enjoy an automated income source.

Chapter 7 - Why Affiliate Programs Are a Good Source of Income

The internet provides all kinds of great opportunities to make money. Affiliate programs are one method of enjoying a good source of income. An added bonus for earning your revenue through this method is that there is no need for you to build a website.

Building a site from scratch is something many don't want to undertake. The idea of having to understand HTML or another foreign language is just more than some of us are willing to undertake. The merchant with the affiliate program(s) takes the difficulty out of it. All you need is a basic site template or a blog and you can start your business.

That's because the merchant provides you with the code you need to sell their product, and in that code I your personal ID, which is how any sales you make are identified. You are provided with the products to sell, which opens up opportunities for many of us who have no products of our own but want to make money online. The affiliate program allows you to take advantage of the hard work of the merchant who provides the product and the ads to market that product, taking a huge burden off of you.

You are also provided with all the marketing material you will need, taking a huge pressure off of you, especially when are first starting out and you haven't generated any revenue to invest in a marketing campaign.

Top-notch affiliate programs provide you with blog articles, banners, graphics, text ads, email campaigns, pay per click keyword campaigns, and a lot more. This provides you with an opportunity to quickly market affiliate products.

How much you make each month is up to you. You can be satisfied with a couple hundred dollars a month, enjoy thousands of dollars or month, or reach for the numbers of an elite few. If you are looking for a full time income, you can do that too.

There is an endless array of affiliate programs to select from – millions to be exact. This means you can choose a niche affiliate that's right for you and you can begin to make money in that niche market. There are many affiliate opportunities online and there are also a number of 2 tier affiliate programs where you will earn residual income. So don't wait another day! Begin to enjoy a good source of income from affiliate programs.

4 Key Areas to Making Money From Affiliate Programs

Your affiliate program has the potential to make money for you as long as you know how to put it all together. Let's have a look at 5 key areas to making money from affiliate programs.

1. Make Sure Your Product, Content, and Visitor is Relevant

One of the most important elements in enjoying a high conversion rate is relevancy. If your visitors are women between the ages of 20 and 25 and you sell women's clothing that targets that age group, then you add men's shoes to the mix as an affiliate.

You shouldn't be surprised if you fail miserably since you have not matched your visitors to your content and the product. Make relevant matches and you will be rewarded with the revenue generation that you were anticipating.

2. Trusting the Affiliate is Critical

There are all kinds of affiliates out there, but it's important that you choose one that you feel comfortable with and trust. That trust extends the other direction as well. Your visitors need to have trust in you, which will increase the likelihood that you will be able to positively market the product(s).

3. Traffic to Your Site or Blog is Key

There are no sales unless you have traffic making it to your site. To increase the likelihood of a conversion you need to bring traffic to the site. The traffic that comes to your site needs to be targeted and relevant. It does you no good to have traffic that's looking for gambling sites when you are selling digital cameras. That's where keywords and search engine optimization come into play. To make money with your affiliate programs you need to put all the components together.

When you offer that targeted traffic a reason to return you convert them and at some point you hope to sell them something. However, in the mean time you'll convert them by offering them something "a free book" "a monthly newsletter" or... well it could be just about anything that's relevant to your site and your affiliate program.

4. Position Yourself

Finally, You need to position yourself. Affiliate programs don't do well if all you do is toss up a banner add across the top of the screen or in the sidebar. Conversion will still happen but not nearly at the rate that conversion occurs if you position your product ads. For example, if you write about a specific product and then include a link to that product within that content your conversion rate will double even triple in some cases.

There you have it – 4 key areas to help you turn your affiliate program into a money making machine.

ABOUT THE AUTHOR

IQ Press, Inc. is a small publishing company dedicated to providing access to educational materials primarily in small business start-up and development. Their mission is to bring the reader useful information that can be implemented with a small capital outlay and generate income streams for the reader to implement.

We trust that you will enjoy these reports and that they will help improve your life.

To get a jumpstart in online marketing download our exclusive quick start guide here:
www.IQPress.org/Quickstart

REFERENCE MATERIALS

Other books you may enjoy to help you on your journey:

Affiliate Marketing for Beginners. Have you heard about affiliate marketing but not quite sure if it's real or really works? This definitive guide will lay out the ins and outs of this interesting field. Filled with tips and hints, it also has information on what to look out for.

Affiliate marketing truly can be started with very little money and has the potential for great rewards. Simple to start with the right guidance, affiliate marketing seriously reduces the risk in starting your own business. Imagine a business with little investment, no inventory, no customer service, no shipping and handling and no risk! Further it can grow to replace your current income and still be operated as a part-time operation. All you need is the enclosed information and you're ready to start.

Affiliate Marketing Secrets: You did become an affiliate marketer to become rich, right? OK, so now what? Start here and learn how to take your fledgling affiliate marketing company to the next step. This report is packed with secret tips and tricks to help you grow your company quickly. After all, your goal is to add customers and new products quickly and expand your business without taking on more risk.

In this short read you will find dozens of ideas to help move your company forward. Not a bunch of theoretical ideas but actual tested tips and techniques to move you towards your goal quickly.

Finding the Best Affiliate Products to Promote: How do I find the best products to sell? Now that you know about affiliate marketing and its great income potential, how can you choose what product(s) to promote? You want one with high demand but not too much competition. You need to choose the category, the product, the venue, the program, etc... That's quite a lot for a new company owner! We can help. This guide will walk you through all these decisions and keep you from getting in a bad place with a product that has poor sell-through.

Available exclusively at: www.IQPress.org

www.ingramcontent.com/pod-product-compliance
Lightning Source LLC
LaVergne TN
LVHW052315060326
832902LV00021B/3896